jordanabeltheplaceofscraps

Praise for *The Place of Scraps*

"With his breakout collection of visual poetry … Abel conjures the near impossible: a heartbreaking history lesson, both personal and public, mixed with lyricism, intelligence, humour, and cold-eyed facts. This narrative of the misguided, good-hearted Marius Barbeau and what he did with First Nations cultural icons will be a revelation for many. What Abel takes from language is what gives it form and strength: a more apt use of plunder verse I cannot imagine."

– CAROLYN SMART

"English litters the sky, its typed letters eventually demolished into illegible insects that flit above archival photo-testimony to land/people … A surprising and necessary book of poetry, *The Place of Scraps* is as humbly unstoppable as the next breath you take in and release back out to the world."

– RITA WONG

"This is art of the concept, used to unmake language so that language may live."

– WAYDE COMPTON

"Abel's textual erasures and collisions manage, all at once, to viscerally enact losses, give voice to silenced histories, make plain the bonds between curation and colonization, reveal cascading ironies, amplify the commentary of mosquitoes. Abel is a master carver of the page."

– SUSAN HOLBROOK

"Astonishingly inventive … Abel's writing constantly dazzles and rewards with its linguistic playfulness and conceptual sophistication."

– ADAM DICKINSON

"*The Place of Scraps* takes on the legacy of the potlatch, an event irresolvably suspended between dynamics of excess and loss, investment and destruction, gift and exchange, general and restricted economies … With sustained attention, serious criticism, and generous respect, Jordan Abel has latched on to the extraordinary luck of lack."

– **CRAIG DWORKIN**

"Abel has broken up Barbeau's text to be examined like any other artifact for its clues of the workings, interactions and exchanges, and contradictions between settler society and Aboriginal society. Yet the 'burden of interpretation' that Abel places on his reader is worth the effort, for there are many moments of insight and beauty."

– **ERIC OSTROWIDZKI**

"An anthropology of anthropology done as only a[n Aboriginal/Indigenous] poet could do."

– **RAY HSU**

"In 1950, Marius Barbeau declared that 'the art of carving poles belongs to the past.' In *The Place of Scraps*, Jordan Abel carves up Barbeau's *Totem Poles*. Scrapping the distinction between literature and sculpture, he reinvents poetry as a plastic art. He is not concerned with finding his own words. He removes Barbeau's. His poems are word-carvings. Some are word-shavings. He simultaneously scraps Barbeau's discourse and conserves it, seizing control of its rules and turning them to new purposes. Ingeniously, his image-texts pass the work of sculpture on to a reader who reads, and rereads, in three dimensions."

– **CHRISTOPHER BRACKEN**

the place of scraps

the place of scraps

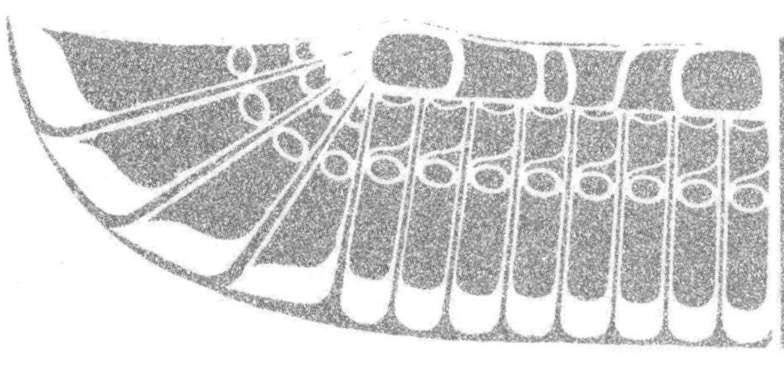

Jordan Abel

Talonbooks

Talonbooks
278 East First Avenue, Vancouver, British Columbia, Canada V5T 1A6
www.talonbooks.com

Second printing: June 2014

Typeset in Minion
Printed and bound in Canada on 100% post-consumer recycled paper

Interior design by Jordan Abel
Cover design by Typesmith

Talonbooks gratefully acknowledges the financial support of the Canada Council for the Arts, the Government of Canada through the Canada Book Fund, and the Province of British Columbia through the British Columbia Arts Council and the Book Publishing Tax Credit.

Library and Archives Canada Cataloguing in Publication

Abel, Jordan, 1985–, author The place of scraps / Jordan Abel.

Poems. ISBN 978-0-88922-788-0 (PBK.)

1. Barbeau, Marius, 1883–1969—Poetry. I. Title.

PS8601.B437P53 2013 C811'.6 C2013-903892-2

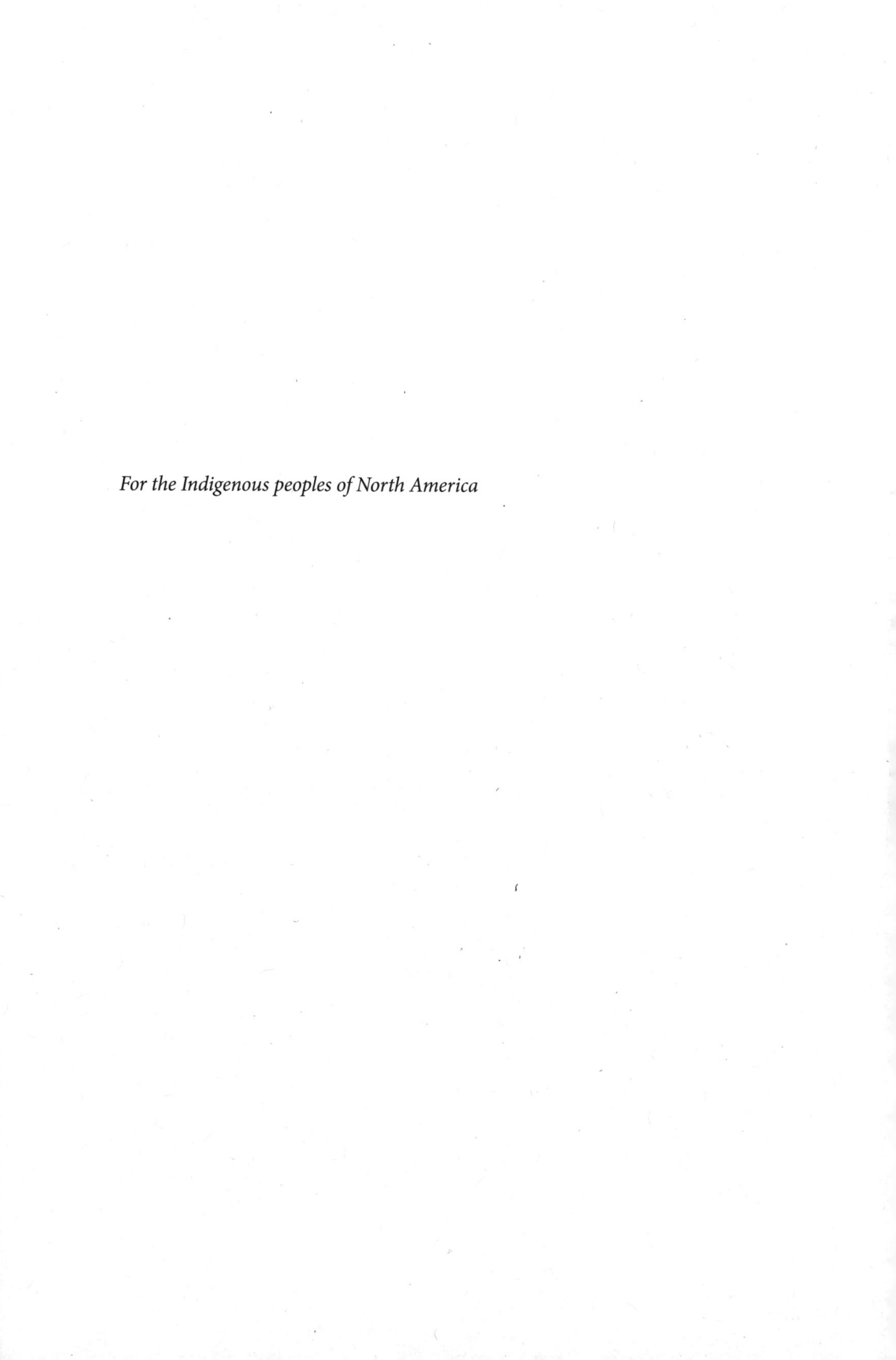

For the Indigenous peoples of North America

1

verthispoleafeudoverthispoleafeudoverthispoleaf
hispoleafeudoverthispoleafeudoverthispoleafeudo
leafeudoverthispoleafeudoverthispoleafeudoverthispo
feudoverthispoleafeudoverthispoleafeudoverthisp
overthispoleafeudoverthispoleafeudoverthispoleaf
verthispoleafeudoverthispoleafeudoverthispoleafeu
hispoleafeudoverthispoleafeudoverthispoleafeudove
oleafeudoverthispoleafeudoverthispoleafeudoverthis
feudoverthispoleafeudoverthispoleafeudoverthispole
overthispoleafeudoverthispoleafeudoverthispoleafeu
verthispoleafeudoverthispoleafeudoverthispoleafeud
hispoleafeudoverthispoleafeudoverthispoleafeudover
oleafeudoverthispoleafeudoverthispoleafeudoverthispole
feudoverthispoleafeudoverthispoleafeudoverthispole
overthispoleafeudoverthispoleafeudoverthispoleafeu
verthispoleafeudoverthispoleafeudoverthispoleafeud
hispoleafeudoverthispoleafeudoverthispoleafeudove
oleafeudoverthispoleafeudoverthispoleafeudoverthis
feudoverthispoleafeudoverthispoleafeudoverthispol
overthispoleafeudoverthispoleafeudoverthispoleafeu
verthispoleafeudoverthispoleafeudoverthispoleafeu
hispoleafeudoverthispoleafeudoverthispoleafeudove
oleafeudoverthispoleafeudoverthispoleafeudoverthi
feudoverthispoleafeudoverthispoleafeudoverthispol
overthispoleafeudoverthispoleafeudoverthispoleafe
verthispoleafeudoverthispoleafeudoverthispoleafeu
hispoleafeudoverthispoleafeudoverthispoleafeudov
oleafeudoverthispoleafeudoverthispoleafeudoverth
feudoverthispoleafeudoverthispoleafeudoverthispo
doverthispoleafeudoverthispoleafeudoverthispoleafe
overthispoleafeudoverthispoleafeudoverthispoleafe
hispoleafeudoverthispoleafeudoverthispoleafeudov
oleafeudoverthispoleafeudoverthispoleafeudoverth
afeudoverthispoleafeudoverthispoleafeudoverthisp
doverthispoleafeudoverthispoleafeudoverthispolea
overthispoleafeudoverthispoleafeudoverthispoleaf
hispoleafeudoverthispoleafeudoverthispoleafeudo
oleafeudoverthispoleafeudoverthispoleafeudoverthis
afeudoverthispoleafeudoverthispoleafeudoverthisp
doverthispoleafeudoverthispoleafeudoverthispolea
overthispoleafeudoverthispoleafeudoverthispolea
hispoleafeudoverthispoleafeudoverthispoleafeud

"*A feud over this pole.* Old chief Mountain or Sakau'wan, some time before his death in 1928, gave an account of the rivalry between the Eagle-Raven clan and the Killer-Whales or Gispewudwades of Nass River, over the size of their new totems.[1] In summary here it is.

The Killer-Whale chief, Sispagut, who headed the faction of the earlier occupants on the river, announced his determination to put up the tallest pole ever seen in the country. Its name was to be Fin-of-the-Killer-Whale. However, instead of selecting for its carver Hladerh whose right it was to do the work, he chose Oyai of the canyon. Hladerh naturally felt slighted and confided his grudge to Sakau'wan, chief of the Eagles, and his friend. From then on the Eagles and the Wolves of their own day were to be closely allied, as the ancestors of both had moved in from Alaska and at one time had been allies.

[1] For a fuller account see *Alaska Beckons* by Marius Barbeau. The Caxton Printers, Caldwell, Idaho and the Macmillan Company of Canada, 1947, pp. 127–136"

Marius Barbeau, *Totem Poles*, vol. 1 (1950), 29.

or Sakau'wan

and

Sispagut
the river
the country

the canyon

allied

by Marius Barbeau

his

new totems

his determination

his
Eagles and Wolves

an account
or
summary

was to be
carve d

from Alaska

his

his

their s[1] h is

h i s h

his i

s

H i s H i s

h i s

his his

h i s

h i s

h i s

[1] For a fuller account see *Alaska Beckons* by Marius Barbeau.

In summary

, his

portedtotorontothepole edtotorontothepoletransportedtotorontothe
ontothepoletransported epo thepoletransportedtotorontothepoletransp
tothepoletransportedt ole poletransportedtotorontothepoletransport
letransportedtotoronto nsport nsportedtotorontothepoletransportedtotor
ransportedtotorontothe ortedt rtedtotorontothepoletransportedtotoron
portedtotorontothepole dtotor otorontothepoletransportedtotorontothe
ntothepoletransporte epole oletransportedtotorontothepoletransp
tothepoletransportedt poletrans etransportedtotorontothepoletransport
letransportedtotoront nsportedto rtedtotorontothepoletransportedtotor
ansportedtotorontoth ortedto totorontothepoletransportedtotoron
portedtotorontothepol dtotorontoth ontothepoletransportedtotorontothe
ntothepoletransporte hepoletransp transportedtotorontothepoletransp
tothepoletransportedt poletransp nsportedtotorontothepoletransport
letransportedtotoront nsportedtotoro ltotorontothepoletransportedtotor
ansportedtotorontoth ortedtotoronto rontothepoletransportedtotoron
ortedtotorontothepo dtotorontothep thepoletransportedtotorontothe
ntothepoletransport hepoletransport portedtotorontothepoletransp
othepoletransported epoletransportedtot rtedtotorontothepoletranspor
etransportedtotoron nsportedtotorontot rontothepoletransportedtotor
ansportedtotorontot portedtotorontothep othepoletransportedtotoron
ortedtotorontothep edtotorontothepoletr oletransportedtotorontothe
ntothepoletransport thepoletransportedto edtotorontothepoletransp
othepoletransporte epoletransportedtotor torontothepoletranspor
etransportedtotor ansportedtotorontothep othepoletransportedtoto
ansportedtotoronto portedtotorontothepole poletransportedtotoron
ortedtotorontothep edtotorontothepoletrans ransportedtotorontothe
ntothepoletranspor thepoletransportedtotoro torontothepoletransp
othepoletransporte hepoletransportedtotoronto ontothepoletranspor
etransportedtotoro ansportedtotorontothepole poletransportedtoto
ansportedtotoronto portedtotorontothepoletra transportedtotoron
ortedtotorontothep edtotorontothepoletransport portedtotorontothe
ntothepoletranspor thepoletransportedtotoronto ntothe letransp
thepoletransporte hepoletransportedtotorontothe thepo spor
transportedtotoro ransportedtotorontothepoletran trans toto
nsportedtotoronto sportedtotorontothepoletransp por
rtedtotorontothep edtotorontothepoletransport
tothepoletranspo thepoletransportedtotorontothe
thepoletransport hepoletransportedtotorontothepo
transportedtotor ransportedtotorontothepoletrans
nsportedtotoront sportedtotorontothe
rtedtotorontothe edtotoront
tothepoletransp
thepoletranspor
transpor dt
nsp

"*The pole transported to Toronto.* To remove this huge totem pole from the Nass, and transfer it to a museum thousands of miles away was not an easy job. Taking it down to the ground and shifting it into the water taxed the ingenuity of a railway engineer and his crew of Indians. It leaned sharply, face forwards, and had it fallen, its carvings would have been damaged. But the work was successfully carried out and after a few days the pole with two others was towed down Portland Canal, on its way south along the coast to Prince Rupert. As it floated in the water, several men could walk on it without feeling a tremor under their feet; it was so large that a few hundred pounds made no difference. When it reached Prince Rupert, it had to be cut, as it lay in the water, into three sections, for the longest railway cars are 50 feet. Nor were all difficulties overcome after the three sections had reached Toronto."

Marius Barbeau, *Totem Poles*, vol. 1 (1950), 34.

remove
transfer
shift

face forwards
work
down
float in
feel
no difference
in the water
or
Toronto

his totem

the water
his Indians

carried
down Portland Canal,

their feet

lay in the water

remove
thousands of

Indians

successfully

without feeling a tremor

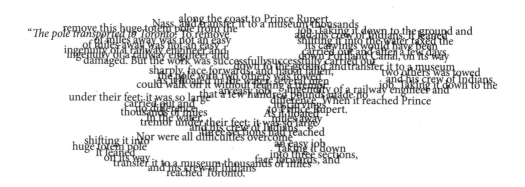

along the coast to Prince Rupert.
Nass, and transfer it to a museum thousands
remove this huge totem pole from the
job. Taking it down to the ground and
“*The pole transported to Toronto.* To remove
and his crew of Indians. It leaned
of miles away was not an easy
shifting it into the water taxed the
of miles away was not an easy
its carvings would have been
ingenuity of a railway engineer and
carried out and after a few days
ingenuity of a railway engineer and
down Portland Canal, on its way
damaged. But the work was successfully
successfully carried out
down to the ground and transfer it to a museum
sharply, face forwards, and had it fallen,
two others was towed
The pole with two others was towed
As it floated in the water, several men
and his crew of Indians.
could walk on it without feeling a tremor
job. Taking it down to the
an easy job
ingenuity of a railway engineer and
under their feet; it was so large
that a few hundred pounds made no
difference. When it reached Prince
carried out and
its carvings
no difference.
to Prince Rupert.
thousands of miles
As it floated
in the water,
miles away
tremor under their feet; it was so large
and his crew of Indians.
three sections had reached
Nor were all difficulties overcome
shifting it into
an easy job
huge totem pole
Taking it down
It leaned
into three sections,
on its way
face forwards, and
transfer it to a museum thousands of miles
and his crew of Indians
reached Toronto.

wanpolefromnassriverremovalofthesakauwanpolefromnassriverremovalofthesakauwanpolefromnassriverremovalofthesakauwanpolefromnassri
npolefromnassriverremovalofthesakauwanpolefromnassriverremovalofthesakauwanpolefromnassriverremovalofthesakauwanpolefromnassriverremova
nassriverremovalofthesakauwanpolefromnassriverremovalofthesakauwanpolefromnassriverremovalofthesakauwanpolefromnassriverremovalofthesak
riverremovalofthesakauwanpolefromnassriverremovalofthesakauwanpolefromnassriverremovalofthesakauwanpolefromnassriverremovalofthesakauwa
rremovalofthesakauwanpolefromnassriverremovalofthesakauwanpolefromnassriverremovalofthesakauwanpolefromnassriverremovalofthesakauwanpol
ovalofthesakauwanpolefromnassriverremovalofthesakauwanpolefromnassriverremovalofthesakauwanpolefromnassriverremovalofthesakauwanpolefro
ofthesakauwanpolefromnassriverremovalofthesakauwanpolefromnassriverremovalofthesakauwanpolefromnassriverremovalofthesakauwanpolefromnas
auwanpolefromnassriverremovalofthesakauwanpolefromnassriverremovalofthesakauwanpolefromnassriverremovalofthesakauwanpolefromnassriverre
wanpolefromnassriverremovalofthesakauwanpolefromnassriverremovalofthesakauwanpolefromnassriverremovalofthesakauwanpolefromnassriverremo
npolefromnassriverremovalofthesakauwanpolefromnassriverremovalofthesakauwanpolefromnassriverremovalofthesakauwanpolefromnassriverremova
nassriverremovalofthesakauwanpolefromnassriverremovalofthesakauwanpolefromnassriverremovalofthesakauwanpolefromnassriverremovalofthesak
riverremovalofthesakauwanpolefromnassriverremovalofthesakauwanpolefromnassriverremovalofthesakauwanpolefromnassriverremovalofthesakauwa
rremovalofthesakauwanpolefromnassriverremovalofthesakauwanpolefromnassriverremovalofthesakauwanpolefromnassriverremovalofthesakauwanpol
ovalofthesakauwanpolefromnassriverremovalofthesakauwanpolefromnassriverremovalofthesakauwanpolefromnassriverremovalofthesakauwanpolefro
ofthesakauwanpolefromnassriverremovalofthesakauwanpolefromnassriverremovalofthesakauwanpolefromnassriverremovalofthesakauwanpolefromnas
auwanpolefromnassriverremovalofthesakauwanpolefromnassriverremovalofthesakauwanpolefromnassriverremovalofthesakauwanpolefromnassriverre
wanpolefromnassriverremovalofthesakauwanpolefromnassriverremovalofthesakauwanpolefromnassriverremovalofthesakauwanpolefromnassriverremo
polefromnassriverremovalofthesakauwanpolefromnassriverremovalofthesakauwanpolefromnassriverremovalofthesakauwanpolefromnassriverremoval
nassriverremovalofthesakauwanpolefromnassriverremovalofthesakauwanpolefromnassriverremovalofthesakauwanpolefromnassriverremovalofthesak
riverremovalofthesakauwanpolefromnassriverremovalofthesakauwanpolefromnassriverremovalofthesakauwanpolefromnassriverremovalofthesakauwa
removalofthesakauwanpolefromnassriverremovalofthesakauwanpolefromnassriverremovalofthesakauwanpolefromnassriverremovalofthesakauwanpole
ovalofthesakauwanpolefromnassriverremovalofthesakauwanpolefromnassriverremovalofthesakauwanpolefromnassriverremovalofthesakauwanpolefro
fthesakauwanpolefromnassriverremovalofthesakauwanpolefromnassriverremovalofthesakauwanpolefromnassriverremovalofthesakauwanpolefromnass
uwanpolefromnassriverremovalofthesakauwanpolefromnassriverremovalofthesakauwanpolefromnassriverremovalofthesakauwanpolefromnassriverrem
wanpolefromnassriverremovalofthesakauwanpolefromnassriverremovalofthesakauwanpolefromnassriverremovalofthesakauwanpolefromnassriverremo
polefromnassriverremovalofthesakauwanpolefromnassriverremovalofthesakauwanpolefromnassriverremovalofthesakauwanpolefromnassriverremoval
nassriverremovalofthesakauwanpolefromnassriverremovalofthesakauwanpolefromnassriverremovalofthesakauwanpolefromnassriverremovalofthesak
riverremovalofthesakauwanpolefromnassriverremovalofthesakauwanpolefromnassriverremovalofthesakauwanpolefromnassriverremovalofthesakauwa
removalofthesakauwanpolefromnassriverremovalofthesakauwanpolefromnassriverremovalofthesakauwanpolefromnassriverremovalofthesakauwanpole
ovalofthesakauwanpolefromnassriverremovalofthesakauwanpolefromnassriverremovalofthesakauwanpolefromnassriverremovalofthesakauwanpolefro
fthesakauwanpolefromnassriverremovalofthesakauwanpolefromnassriverremovalofthesakauwanpolefromnassriverremovalofthesakauwanpolefromnass
uwanpolefromnassriverremovalofthesakauwanpolefromnassriverremovalofthesakauwanpolefromnassriverremovalofthesakauwanpolefromnassriverrem
anpolefromnassriverremovalofthesakauwanpolefromnassriverremovalofthesakauwanpolefromnassriverremovalofthesakauwanpolefromnassriverremov
polefromnassriverremovalofthesakauwanpolefromnassriverremovalofthesakauwanpolefromnassriverremovalofthesakauwanpolefromnassriverremoval
assriverremovalofthesakauwanpolefromnassriverremovalofthesakauwanpolefromnassriverremovalofthesakauwanpolefromnassriverremovalofthesaka
iverremovalofthesakauwanpolefromnassriverremovalofthesakauwanpolefromnassriverremovalofthesakauwanpolefromnassriverremovalofthesakauwan
emovalofthesakauwanpolefromnassriverremovalofthesakauwanpolefromnassriverremovalofthesakauwanpolefromnassriverremovalofthesakauwanpolef
valofthesakauwanpolefromnassriverremovalofthesakauwanpolefromnassriverremovalofthesakauwanpolefromnassriverremovalofthesakauwanpolefrom
thesakauwanpolefromnassriverremovalofthesakauwanpolefromnassriverremovalofthesakauwanpolefromnassriverremovalofthesakauwanpolefromnassr
wanpolefromnassriverremovalofthesakauwanpolefromnassriverremovalofthesakauwanpolefromnassriverremovalofthesakauwanpolefromnassriverremo
anpolefromnassriverremovalofthesakauwanpolefromnassriverremovalofthesakauwanpolefromnassriverremovalofthesakauwanpolefromnassriverremov
olefromnassriverremovalofthesakauwanpolefromnassriverremovalofthesakauwanpolefromnassriverremovalofthesakauwanpolefromnassriverremovalo
assriverremovalofthesakauwanpolefromnassriverremovalofthesakauwanpolefromnassriverremovalofthesakauwanpolefromnassriverremovalofthesaka
verremovalofthesakauwanpolefromnassriverremovalofthesakauwanpolefromnassriverremovalofthesakauwanpolefromnassriverremovalofthesakauwanp
emovalofthesakauwanpolefromnassriverremovalofthesakauwanpolefromnassriverremovalofthesakauwanpolefromnassriverremovalofthesakauwanpolef
valofthesakauwanpolefromnassriverremovalofthesakauwanpolefromnassriverremovalofthesakauwanpolefromnassriverremovalofthesakauwanpolefro
hesakauwanpolefromnassriverremovalofthesakauwanpolefromnassriverremovalofthesakauwanpolefromnassriverremovalofthesakauwanpolefromnas
wanpolefromnassriverremovalofthesakauwanpolefromnassriverremovalofthesakauwanpolefromnassriverremovalofthesakauwanpolefromnassriverre
anpolefromnassriverremovalofthesakauwanpolefromnassriverremovalofthesakauwanpolefromnassriverremovalofthesakauwanpolefromnassriverremo
olefromnassriverremovalofthesakauwanpolefromnassriverremovalofthesakauwanpolefromnassriverremovalofthesakauwanpolefromnassriverremova
assriverremovalofthesakauwanpolefromnassriverremovalofthesakauwanpolefromnassriverremovalofthesakauwanpolefromnassriverremovalofthesaka
rremovalofthesakauwanpolefromnassriverremovalofthesakauwanpolefromnassriverremovalofthesakauwanpolefromnassriverremovalofthesakauwa
ovalofthesakauwanpolefromnassriverremovalofthesakauwanpolefromnassriverremovalofthesakauwanpolefromnassriverremovalofthesakauwanpol
fthesakauwanpolefromnassriverremovalofthesakauwanpolefromnassriverremovalofthesakauwanpolefromnassriverremovalofthesakauwanpolefro
mnassriverremovalofthesakauwanpolefromnassriverremovalofthesakauwanpolefromnassriverremovalofthesakauwanpolefromnas
sriverremovalofthesakauwanpolefromnassriverremovalofthesakauwanpolefromnassriverre
erremovalofthesakauwanpolefromnassriverremovalofthesakauwanpolefromnassriverremo
movalofthesakauwanpolefromnassriverremovalofthesakauwanpolefromnassriverremova
npolefromnassriverremovalofthesakauwanpolefromnassriverremovalofthesaka
movalofthesakauwanpolefromnassriverremovalofthesakauwa
lefromnassriverremovalofthesakauwanpol
riverremovalofthesakauwanp efro
emovalofthes

"*Removal of the Sakau'wan pole from Nass River.* The totem pole of the Mountain Eagle at Gitiks, a deserted village on the lower Nass, was the tallest and finest on the Northwest Coast. It stood for something memorable in the life of many Indians, a symbol of prehistoric America with its wild animals and its dusky tribes, and of a supreme effort to express nature in terms of human interest. For sheer stateliness it seemed unsurpassed anywhere as a work of native art and stylisation. Its many figures of animals, beautifully carved, mounted on one another into the sky. They formed a splendid and uniform structure, all out of the trunk of one giant red cedar of Portland Canal. The proud Eagle of the mountains, or the Thunderbird, was perched at the summit. Lost in the jungle of the lower Nass, close to the Alaskan border, I first saw this totem in 1927, as it leaned precariously on two props over the bank of the river. The forest all around was gradually reclaiming its rights after the native villagers had departed many years ago for other haunts, or had died out."

Marius Barbeau, *Totem Poles*, vol. 1 (1950), 32.

his

stateliness

a splendid

summit

over

the villagers

the Northwest Coast

express

ed

to

the

border

hung over
the fire
propped up

poked at

for

the
sight of

the
world

The anthropologist humbled by beauty and the sleepless moon. Even though we had taken enough food for two weeks, I could not eat the meal that Barton had prepared. The moon hung low, barely visible over the tops of the trees, and I found myself staring into the fire, pondering the significance of what I had seen today. The sight of that pole propped up over running water nagged at my conscience. At any point the great pole could topple into the river, and I would have been the last one to see it, the last one to truly understand its beauty.

The gas boat swayed in the water; the tent billowed in the breeze; the village by the river's edge remained deserted; the pole inched closer to the ground. Barton poked at the fire, sending orange sparks into the air. How could I deprive the rest of the world from this wondrous treasure? How could I deprive the future generations of this gift? Anyone with a sound mind and a respectable education would understand that this monument must be preserved, and that I am bound by duty to be the one to preserve it.

thesilhouetteofapoleontheshoreofnassriver

"The pole of 'Neesyoq and 'Neeskyinwæt, members of a Wolf clan at Gitlarhdamks, on upper Nass River. It stood seventh from the uppermost in the row of poles along the river front.

Description. It stood in front of a house called House-of-the-Sky (*wilplarhæ*) and belonged to the *ptsæn* type (hollow-back and carved all over). Its figures, from top to bottom, are: (1) mythical man with the deep sea cockle adhering to a rock (*kal'own*) holding his hand fast—illustrating a myth; (2) the head of the Sperm Whale (*hlpoon*), the jaw hanging down; (3) Person (*gyet*) wearing a garment with many faces on it, probably the Garment-of-Marten (*gwisha'dao'tk*); (4) the bird Gyaibelk, at the bottom of the pole. This mythical bird was also used as a head-dress (*amhallait*) and as a spirit (*narhnorh* or *narhnok*).

Function, carver, age. Erected in memory of a former 'Neesyoq by the present (in 1927) chief of the same name, an old man. It no longer exists. Carved by Paræt'Nærhl, assisted by his son, about eighty years ago.

(Informant, Dennis Wood of Gitlarhdamks.)"

Marius Barbeau, *Totem Poles*, vol. 2 (1950), 442.

(*wilplarhæ*) (
) ( )
(*kal'own*)
( ) (*hlpoon*)
( ) (*gyet*)
(*gwisha'dao'tk*) ( )
(*amhallait*)
(*narhnorh* *narhnok*)

( )

( )

(field)

(process wherein

language readjusts to

)

( )

(casualty)

( )

(a description of

)

(

all)

The silhouette of a pole on the shore of Nass River. When I was satisfied with the day (field notes completed) and when my ears were sufficiently exhausted by the translations (a process wherein an informant evaluates the qualities of a speech in one language and readjusts them to suit another language), I made my way back to the river. The branches from the trees overhead dipped onto the path (noteable), and the needles bristled against my palms (a casualty of the ethnological process).

My informant (Dennis Wood), caught up with me at the bank of the river. He was out of breath, offering up my notebook in his hands. "You forgot this," he said, handing the book back to me. This gesture (a description of a bodily action) took me a moment to comprehend, but once I gathered myself, I patted him on the back and said, "Thank you." This affirmation was not lost on him, as he began to speak at once about the crested column that stood against the river. He explained that the man on the top was telling a story, and I gathered that he was comparing me to this man (as I had been endeavouring to learn all of their stories). Although I knew that I must be nothing like this man, I was flattered all the same, and did not object as my informant continued to speak.

13.07.1992

The poet, deep in a docile state of youth, is transported to Toronto by his mother. Simultaneously, the correct stimuli and trajectory of thought trigger formations of memory—rattling, fluorescent subway cars; bleached sky over Bloor Street; hinged glass doors opening into the Royal Ontario Museum. The poet is mapped onto a web of simulation populated by artifact and orchestration. The poet obeys the rules (contemplative lingering, artificial glimmers of insight) as though a violation would be severely punished. The poet endures—level one, stairwell; level two, stairwell; level three, stairwell; level four, stairwell. But the poet is incapable of converting the contents of the stairwell into memory; the poet does not identify the totem pole in the stairwell as the pole erected by Sakau'wan, the same pole that was removed from the Nass River valley in three pieces by Marius Barbeau.

25.07.1990

xd g c
t l l r r m t
n d t s q r
g p n t l n n w m
t f r b r þ
g s l v h r d
s w h s r
v l x c h
m n p
p

25.12.2010

The poet exchanges gifts with his family; he gives his mother a book, a graphic novel, which is read immediately. The poet's mother identifies a section of the text and indicates that the page in question is a shared component of their past. The page depicts a totem pole in the Royal Ontario Museum. The poet's mother inquires if he remembers being there. But the poet does not hold that memory. The poet simply recalls the train car and the heat. Momentarily, the poet is surprised and ashamed that the pole that was removed from his ancestral village has also been excavated from his own memories. The situation defuses quickly, anticlimactically. But the recurrence of the totem pole in the poet's life combined with an apparent failure of memory carries with it a multiplicity of subtle emotions.

"*The myth of the Dragon-Fly.* A young unmarried woman of this clan, whose name was Yaw'l, broke her seclusion taboos to play with her brothers. Although it was summertime, a heavy fall of snow covered the ground at night. When the brothers and sister looked outside, they found themselves in a strange country; their house was nearly covered with snow. Huge-Belly, a monstrous being, appeared from time to time, calling the young taboo-breakers outside, one by one, in order to cut them open with his long, sharp, glass-like nose, and hang their bodies on the rafters of his lodge to smoke and dry like split salmon. One of them managed to kill him. The slayer took to flight with his sister and remaining brothers, but to little avail. A female being of the same kind, Ksemkaigyet, who could draw out her nose into a sharp knife, pursued them. As they hid in a tree at the edge of a lake, she detected their shadows in the frosty waters and dived several times to capture them, until she was quite frozen. Then they killed her. But before she died, she declared, "The people will always suffer from my nose." From her remains were born the mosquitoes and other pests."

Marius Barbeau, *Totem Poles*, vol. 1 (1950), 24.

. this clan
’, .
, covered the ground
. ,
; covered .
time
, , with , ,
, smoke
. .
and , .
, ,
.
, shadows
, .
, ,
. .
, :

'

.   .

’,

,

.

;

one by one
their bodies
split
with
the kind ,
knife .

,

, .

, ,

.

, :

summertime

in a strange country;
time
with

the
remaining

and
the

remains

broke   n

, calling

the   smoke

the   water
the
people

time   calling

the

people

with sand with blood

with smoke

with
snow

their inner workings
filled with

a ravenous hunger

the language

of

a strange country.

the solitude
opened
with
Ksemkaigyet's

palms
the smoke

once more
in the woods

.

,   .

,   his work

their   working

.

a   .

.

specimen

. .

held in

.   spirit

.

.

, .

, split open

, .

. fill , in

,

. .

.

.

. ,

.

. what had happened

and .

had become

,

. .

The Tale of the Blacked-Out Sky at Noon. That winter the snow had blanketed the Nass River Valley, but the old man Ksemkaigyet barely noticed. He had secluded himself from the village, found comfort in the solitude of his work—spliting open dragonflies, determining their inner workings. But each specimen he opened revealed something different. Some were filled with sand, others with blood or pine needles. He allowed himself to crack open only one each day. But Ksemkaigyet's desire to know how they worked soon became a ravenous hunger. And he found himself spliting open every specimen he had until he came upon one dragonfly that was filled with smoke—wreaths upon wreaths—and ice water. Ksemkaigyet was stunned. The smoking creature he held in his palms was not a dragonfly at all, but a spirit in disguise. The glass-nosed spirit rose from the smoke and spoke in a language that he did not understand. But before Ksemkaigyet knew what had happened the spirit transformed into a dragonfly once more and flew out of the lodge. He followed the spirit out into the woods and saw that the sky had become blackened with the beating wings of dragonflies, that all those wings together were melting all of the snow. He had indeed found himself in a strange country.

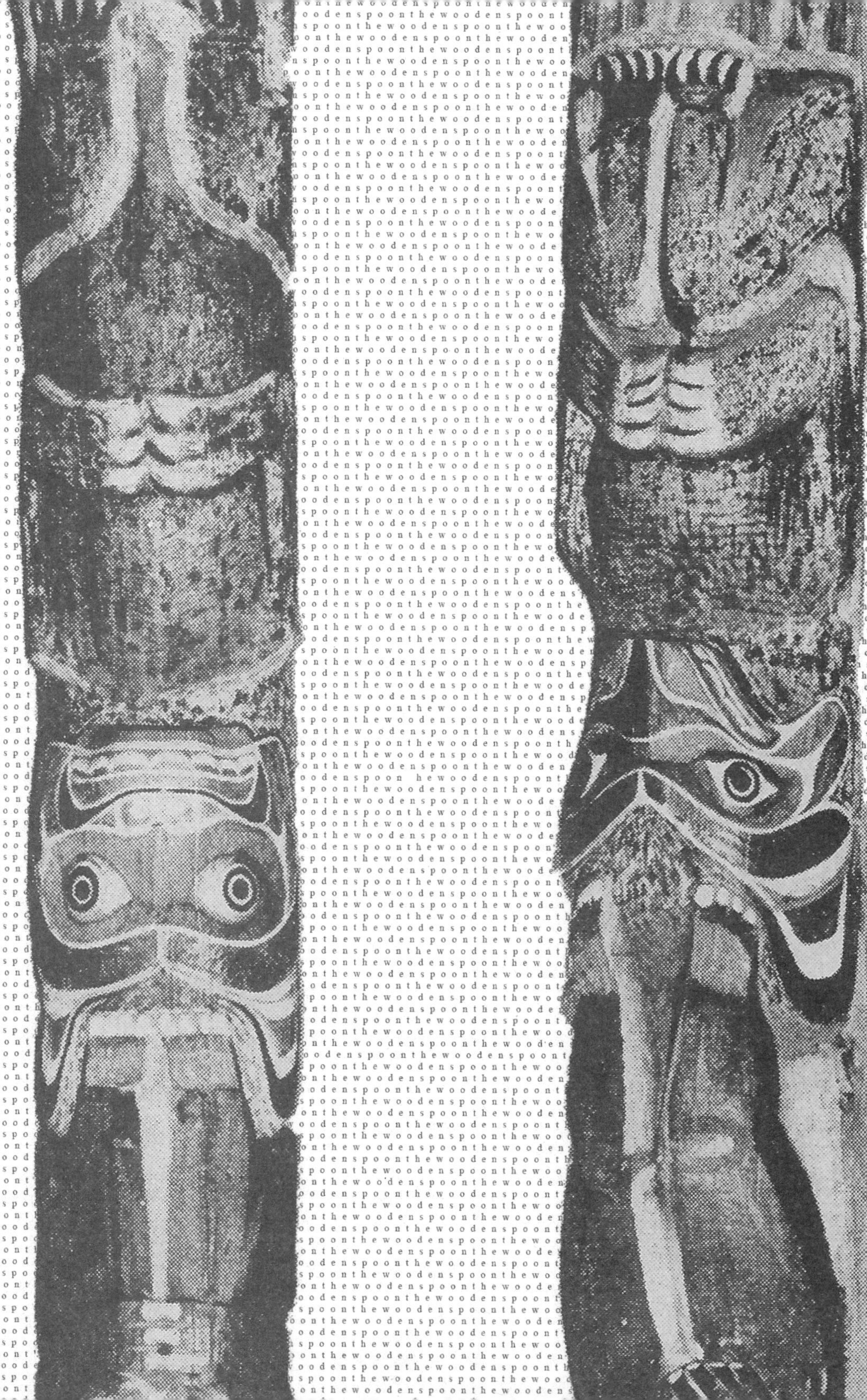

12.06.2008

The poet returns to Vancouver, his birth city, after a twenty-one year absence. The poet investigates the last known locations of his father; the poet internalizes the procedures of the city; the poet exchanges premeditated extrapolations for physical grandiosity. The city indulges the poet's weakness for vegetation and water-adjacent sand; the city believes in the authenticity of beauty and strategically located totem poles. The poet arranges a meeting with the former friends of his parents who attempt to explain the truth behind the theatricality of his infancy. The former friends of his parents give the poet a wooden spoon that his absent father carved. The poet initiates the suitable gestures for thankfulness and rotates the spoon over and over in his palms.

12.06.2008

c

t

g n

b

d

x

n w

s

26.06.2008

n c v

p

d t

g n m

b c

j f n d

x s r

n pw

sf

.

26.06.2008

n v
p
d
m
c
j f n
s r
p
f

26.06.2008

The poet travels back to Edmonton and reassesses the validity of his knowledge of the past. The poet rotates the wooden spoon in his hands and becomes distracted by its history: unblemished, unused. He contemplates putting the spoon to use, but finding himself unable to do so, places the wooden spoon on the shelf. Without warning, the poet becomes acutely aware of his own projected purpose for the wooden spoon, an object designed for the uncontrollable nakedness of spectacle. The poet takes an inventory of all of the similar pieces he has witnessed: the totem pole in the mall, the emblems on the manhole covers, the endless carvings for sale in Water Street storefronts, and the wooden spoon on the shelf.

"*Myth explaining some of the crests* (Chief Mountain's version). The ancestral myth of the Gitrhawn (Salmon-Eater) clan gives the following account: After the canoes of the people had travelled down the coast a long way from the North, they landed at a place called Ahlknebært, south of Stikine River. They were close to Marhla'angyesawmks (now called Tongas Narrows). As the sockeye salmon were plentiful here they fished, caught some, and cooked them ashore. The day was warm. Gunas, a nephew of the chief, went into the salt water to swim. His fellows saw a large halibut come up and swallow him. They hunted around and watched, hoping to find traces of the fish. Soon they beheld the Eagle at the edge of the water, and close to it, the great Halibut. They caught the Halibut, cut it open, and found the remains of their kinsman inside. His flesh was already partly decayed, and he had a copper ring around his neck. The father of the dead Gunas stood at the head of the Halibut and started to cry: "This is the place of the Spirit Halibut." It became a dirge, to be remembered ever after. They burned the body and hastened on their journey south."

Marius Barbeau, *Totem Poles*, vol. 1 (1950), 52.

follow
the coast

cut open

the dead
place

the

sockeye
shore
the salt
hunt

the
flesh
around
the Spirit

the
remains of
a
head

found
decayed,

account:

the

plentiful
day

already

burned

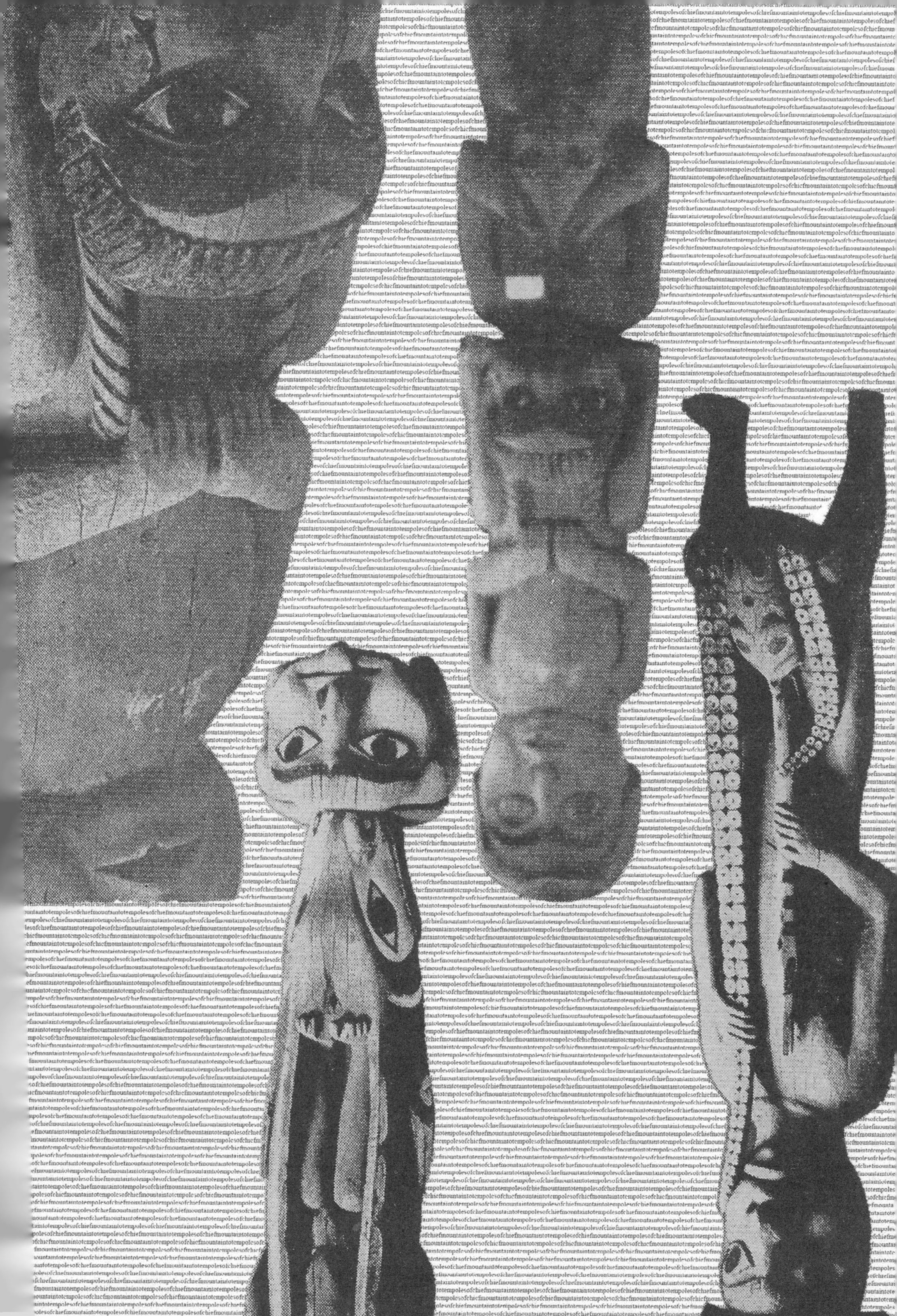

"*Totem Poles of Chief Mountain (Boas)* (111b: 573, 574). Some time after a burial the son or nephew of the deceased erects a column in his memory (*ptsan*). As the meaning of such is not yet clear by any means, I asked 'Chief Mountain' to describe to me the festivals which he gave after the death of his father, who was a Gyispawaduwada. His father had a squid for his protector (*nagnok*). After the death of his father he invited all the people to his house. During the festival the ground opened and a huge rock, which was covered with kelp, came out. This was made of wood and bark. A cave was under the rock and a large squid came out of it. It was made of cedar bark and its arms were set with hooks which caught the blankets of the audience and tore them. The song of the squid was sung by the women sitting on three platforms in the rear of the house."

Marius Barbeau, *Totem Poles*, vol. 1 (1950), 35.

the deceased
(meaning
the
Gyispawaduwada
)

came out
squid
set with hooks

meaning

his father

covered with kelp,

made of cedar bark

and song

ground open

the rock

tore the
platform

and

sung

“

column
clear

cave

blankets

squid
house”

the son or
is not yet clear describe to me the
the festival the ground in the rear of
rock and a large squid the death of
after a burial by any means
After the death of his is not yet clear
squid was sung the death of
on three platforms the rock and a large
is not yet clear is not yet clear
is not yet clear the son or
is not yet clear
After the death of his

the rock and a large
Chief Mountain to
after a burial who was a
the rock and a large the son or
was made of wood (*nagnok*). After the
After the death of his which was covered with kelp,
e rock and a large came out. This was
the son or (*nagnok*). After the
the rock and the son or
is not yet clear rock and a large squid
the son or is not yet clear
his house.

is not yet clear (*nagnok*). After the
the death of his is not yet clear
is not yet clear he invited all
the rock and a large who was a
the son or the son or
he invited all the rock and a large
after a burial he invited all
he invited all kelp came
audience and to his house
opened and a huge
Gyispawaduwada

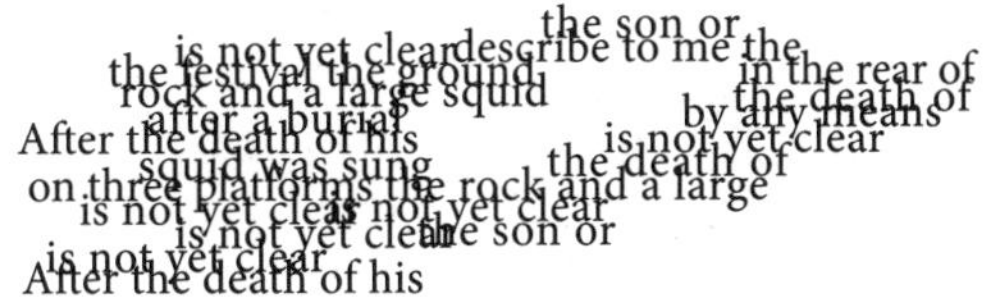

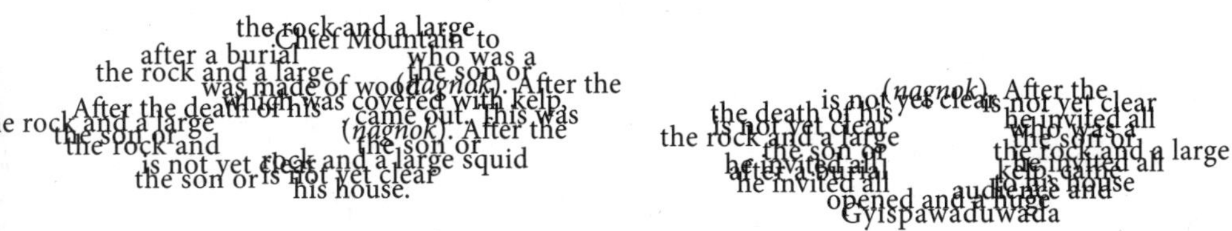

istoriesthemilkofhypotheticalhistoriesthemilkofhypotheticalhistoriesthemilk
toriesthemilkofhypotheticalhistoriesthemilkofhypotheticalhistoriesthemilkof
kofhypotheticalhistoriesthemilkofhypotheticalhistoriesthemilkofhypothetical
heticalhistoriesthemilkofhypotheticalhistoriesthemilkofhypotheticalhistories
calhistoriesthemilkofhypotheticalhistoriesthemilkofhypotheticalhistoriesthe
istoriesthemilkofhypotheticalhistoriesthemilkofhypotheticalhistoriesthemil
toriesthemilkofhypotheticalhistoriesthemilkofhypotheticalhistoriesthemil
kofhypotheticalhistoriesthemilkofhypotheticalhistoriesthemilkofhypot
heticalhistoriesthemilkofhypotheticalhistoriesthemilkofhypotheticalh
calhistoriesthemilkofhypotheticalhistoriesthemilkofhypotheticalhisto

21.04.1985
The infant poet, a blank slate, refuses to submit to the procedures of childhood, cries out with and against the air around him. He tests the limits of his circumstances with his extremities. But lacking in dextral confidence, he resigns his free will to the patterns of others. He is frustrated by the painful construction of days: bright light, catharsis, bright light. He does not comprehend that his father is deep within the process of carving a canoe with his fellow carvers so that they can follow the coast up from Vancouver to the Nass. He does not understand that his father carves totem poles to sell to tourists, paints on canvases for the storefronts of Water Street. He cannot define the tradition that his father functions within.

05.04.1985

h r w b

ms b t s

f m x d x f h

p k n t v

d q sh n h

t c h wb

m s r t

r h

05.08.2011

Of his own volition, the poet returns to Toronto, confident that he will be reunited with the totem pole removed from the Nass River valley by Marius Barbeau. The poet confronts the admissions staff member at the ROM, explains that he refuses to pay to see a totem pole that was taken from his ancestral village. The staff member initiates a lethargic request to allow admission under special circumstances but is unable to contact any of his superiors. The staff member shrugs, verbalizes his apathy, and allows the poet into the museum. The pole towers through the staircase; the poet circles up to the top. The pole is here; the poet is here.

05.04.1985

w

m t

f m x

n t v

d c

t w

m s t

r h

05.04.1989

w

t

f

d

c

05.04.1985

2a

translated
“ shadow

of stars.”

barren

fist

an endless
hike
through
the wind.

"There are no poles here."

I trudged on

I translated

I rested I caught I gazed

I must remember

The place of scraps. I trudged on behind Barton, barely lifting my feet over the roots that muscled their way out of the forest floor. Barton spoke in Niskae and in endless breath about our destination—the place of scraps—and I translated what I could as we hiked. "Two moons." Brushed by pine needles. "The shadow of." Filtered light through the canopy. "His grandson." Salted air. "At peace with the wind." A clearing up ahead. "To Sakau'wan." At long last. "The trail of stars." The clearing.

I rested against the moss trunk of a great tree. I caught my wind. I gazed at Barton as he ventured into the middle of the barren circle. In English, he said, "There are no poles here." He kneeled and his hand disappeared into the ground. After a moment, he withdrew a fistful of dirt and shavings of wood. He said, "Hold out your hands." So I did. And he sifted the mulch into my palms. He was silent as the last clumps of dirt left his fingers, and I knew then, standing in that sunstruck clearing, that this was a sacred ritual, that I must remember each detail so that the world could know it, too.

Primitive culture circulates within the spirit of charm. As does the mediation by a spiritual agent. Whose labour itself is so monotonous that slight variations often go unnoticed.

The *of* I on behind Barton, barely lifting my feet over the that their out of the forest floor. Barton spoke in and breath our destination—the place of and I what as we hiked. "Two moons." Brushed by needles. "The of." Filtered light the canopy. "His grandson." air. "At peace with the wind." A clearing up ahead. "To " At long last. "The trail of stars." The clearing.

I against the trunk of a great tree. I caught my wind. I gazed at Barton as he ventured into the middle of the barren circle. In English, he said, "There are no poles here." He kneeled and his hand disappeared into the ground. After a moment, he withdrew a fistful of dirt and shavings of wood. He said, "Hold out your hands." So I did. And he sifted the mulch into my palms. He was silent as the last clumps of dirt left his fingers, and I knew then, standing in that sunstruck clearing, that this was a sacred ritual, that I must remember each detail so that the world could know it, too.

In practice, the civilized world is obstructed by their determination. The mere mention of acquisition results in the most savage attention: rich detail of experience, unintentional formality.

The of I on Barton, lifting over the that their Barton spoke in and breath destination and I what as we moons rushed by needles. "The of." light the canopy grandson." air. "At peace ." A ahead. "To " At long last. "The trail of stars." The clearing.

I against the trunk of a tree. I caught my wind. I gazed at Barton as he ventured into the middle of the barren . In English, he said, "There are no poles here." He kneeled and his hand disappeared into the ground. After a moment, he withdrew a fistful of dirt and shavings of wood. He said, "Hold out your hands." So I did. And he sifted the mulch into my palms. He was silent as the last clumps of dirt left his fingers, and I knew then, standing in that sunstruck clearing, that this was a sacred ritual, that I must remember each detail so that the world could know it, too.

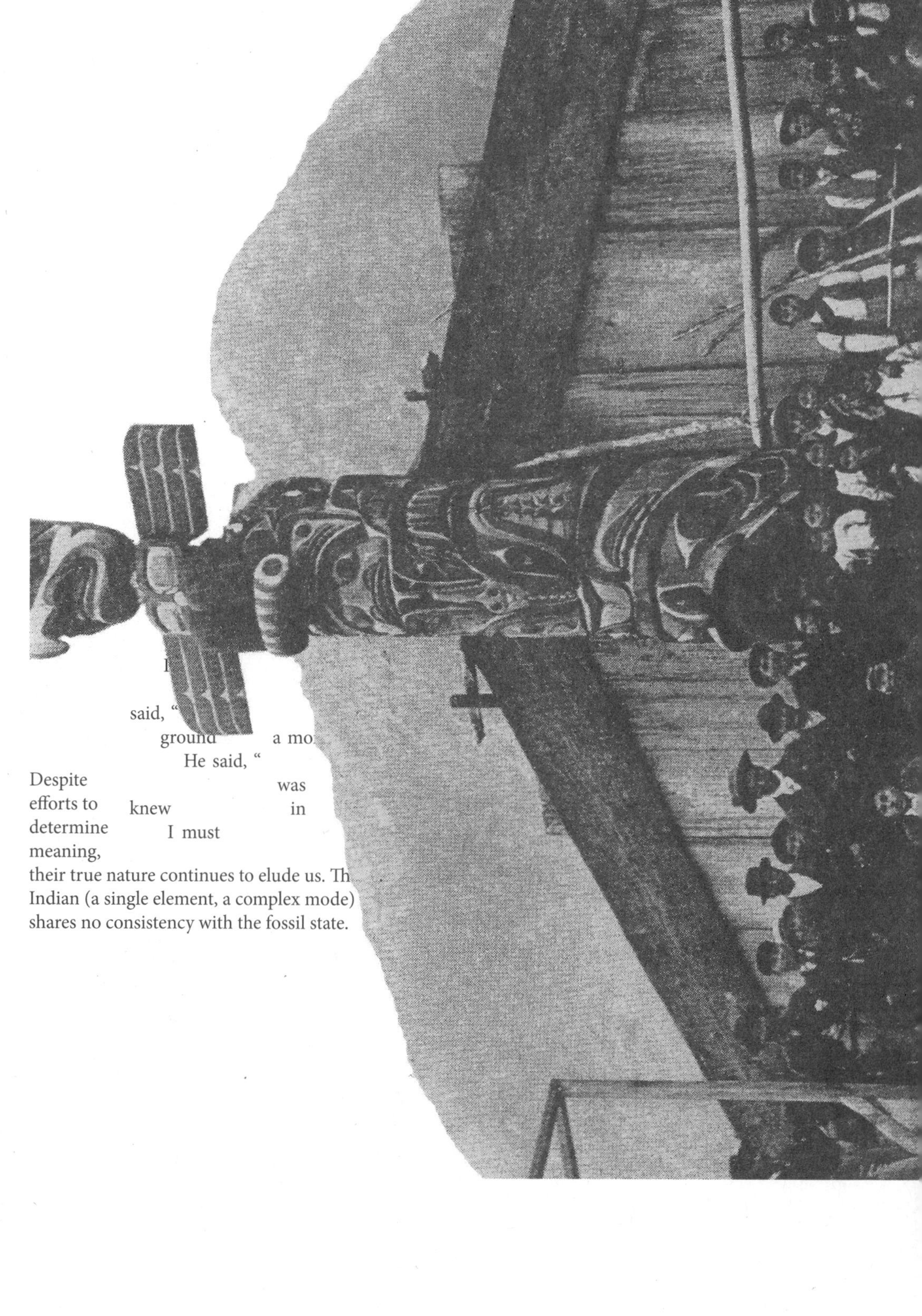

I

said, “

ground a mo

He said, “

Despite was

efforts to knew in

determine I must

meaning,

their true nature continues to elude us. Th

Indian (a single element, a complex mode)

shares no consistency with the fossil state.

The *of* I on Barton, lifting
that their
in and destination
what as we moons rushed
by needles. " of. light
." air. " " A ahead. "To
" ." The
I trunk gazed
as he into the of the In
said, " hand into
ground a moment withdrew of dirt of
He said, " did the
was as clumps his and
knew in sunstruck this was
I must so the world too.

Contact is precisely the investigation that we endevoured to embark upon. The frequency in which their values are reassigned is the mark of the future, and it should be crossed again and again.

culture spirit world by
charm the mere of
results savage
that
The *of* Barton, lifting experience,
that
. in and destination

“

. .”

the
was his and
efforts knew in
I must world too.

true nature elude embark frequency
Indian element, values is the
no consistency be . and

coffinhouseofthefrogcoffinhouseofthefrogcoffinhouseofthefrog

"Coffin Hous[illegible]*rog.* The F[illegible] crest connected with the Bear crest in the "C[illegible] of the frog [illegible]", as recorded by James Deans, 36: 55, 56).

This story, a[illegible]nnected with [illegible] Choo[illegible]za-ton or bear crest, is the only one in [illegible] far as I have [illegible]en abl[illegible] to learn, connected with the Kimquestan[illegible] crest. I have [illegible]en to[illegible] that this was a secret society belongi[illegible]y to women[illegible]his [illegible]ciety had their "coffin house of the fr[illegible]*hling-nak-kimq*[illegible]*an*); [illegible] have been inside of it. Having seen it, [illegible] description of [illegible] Whe[illegible] I saw it in the summer of 1883, it was [illegible]ilt of cedar [illegible]ks, [illegible]losing a space twenty feet square. Its [illegible]rly flat and cov[illegible]d w[illegible] cedar boards. Right in the centre of th[illegible]d a huge [illegible]oode[illegible]rog. [illegible]orming a square around this frog and s[illegible]t on each [illegible]e p[illegible]d, one above the other, fifty or sixty co[illegible] boxes of [illegible] an[illegible] sizes. I[illegible] each one were the dried-up r[illegible] human b[illegible] s[illegible]y is f[illegible]om the Queen Charlotte Island[illegible]

Marius Barbeau[illegible] vol. 1 (195[illegible] 78[illegible]).

This story

is a secret

I have been inside of

Rubric unknown: understand every
type of law and government, language
and thought. Or else hindered in their
speculation
other clues,
namely,
our far-off
origins. This story

was

built

from
coffins

counteract the active
ide the thousands of
owards a sharp knife,
as if
teeth had
their cores
lying
about.

the

flat

This story

The third is
and last
golden age
of art: with
the ashes
of the department preserving alcoves
of red ochre—from some religious
mutilation—the menagerie is suspect.

Let us
proceed
through
the
modern,
to the swarm of abundance. The world
by now a high plateu over the varied
woodlanders, the men of the sea.

"Had the old Indian been aware of modern trends among his people, he might have acted otherwise and provided for his own grave and tombstone, as did another veteran of the same clan—chief Grizzly-Bear (*Samedeek*), of Kitwanga, on the Skeena river. Grizzly-Bear some years ago felt that death had come to his door, for he was old and very ill. He summoned his nephews, and had his grave built around him, in his very house-tomb, tombstone, posts, wire fence and all. He paid for the materials and services with ancient gold coins, for he did not think that his heirs would bother much with his remains after his death; carved totems no longer being erected to the memory of uncles. The first night after his installation in the midst of his grave, he slept in his tomb. But he failed to die. I saw him next summer slowly walking the trail down to the river. Come what may, his dignified rest was assured. The lot of Mountain, his relative on the Nass, was to be buried without honours in the common village plot."

Marius Barbeau, *Totem Poles*, vol. 1 (1950), 33.

We have scarcely begun to illustrate the
remains of the earliest races. While others stand
still, or even decay, we time "total services,"
which,
moreover,
are the
doctrine
of the
Indian
prophet.

and provided

veteran of the

door, for he

in his very

did not think that his heirs

It is even incorrect to speak of their nearest
parallels. We are here. Logical causes may be
given. But any given institution, lump of lead,
river foam,
etc. gives rise
to actions,
social
practices—
however
slight.

otherwise and provided

of the same clan

years ago felt

around him

services with ancient

carved totems no longer

he failed to die

Mountain, his relative

(Samedeek)

(Samedeek)

wire fence and all

wire fence and all

Physical
actions
are
expected.
Every
mountain
ash, birch,
sacred fig, camphor, incense differs in regards to fertility. In reality, these pieces of "property" see no consistency.

his installation in the midst

his installation in the midst

to the river

to the river

village plot.

village plot.

old Indian
old Indian

Skeena river
Skeena river

the materials
the materials

in the midst
in the midst

summer slowly
summer slowly

was to be buried
was to be buried

At least this
functions
among the
magical
rites of the
Kwakiutl,
the Haida.
The rudeness of their life seems to us appalling, as
an animal capable of ritual who cannot escape the
residue of sympathetic social patterns

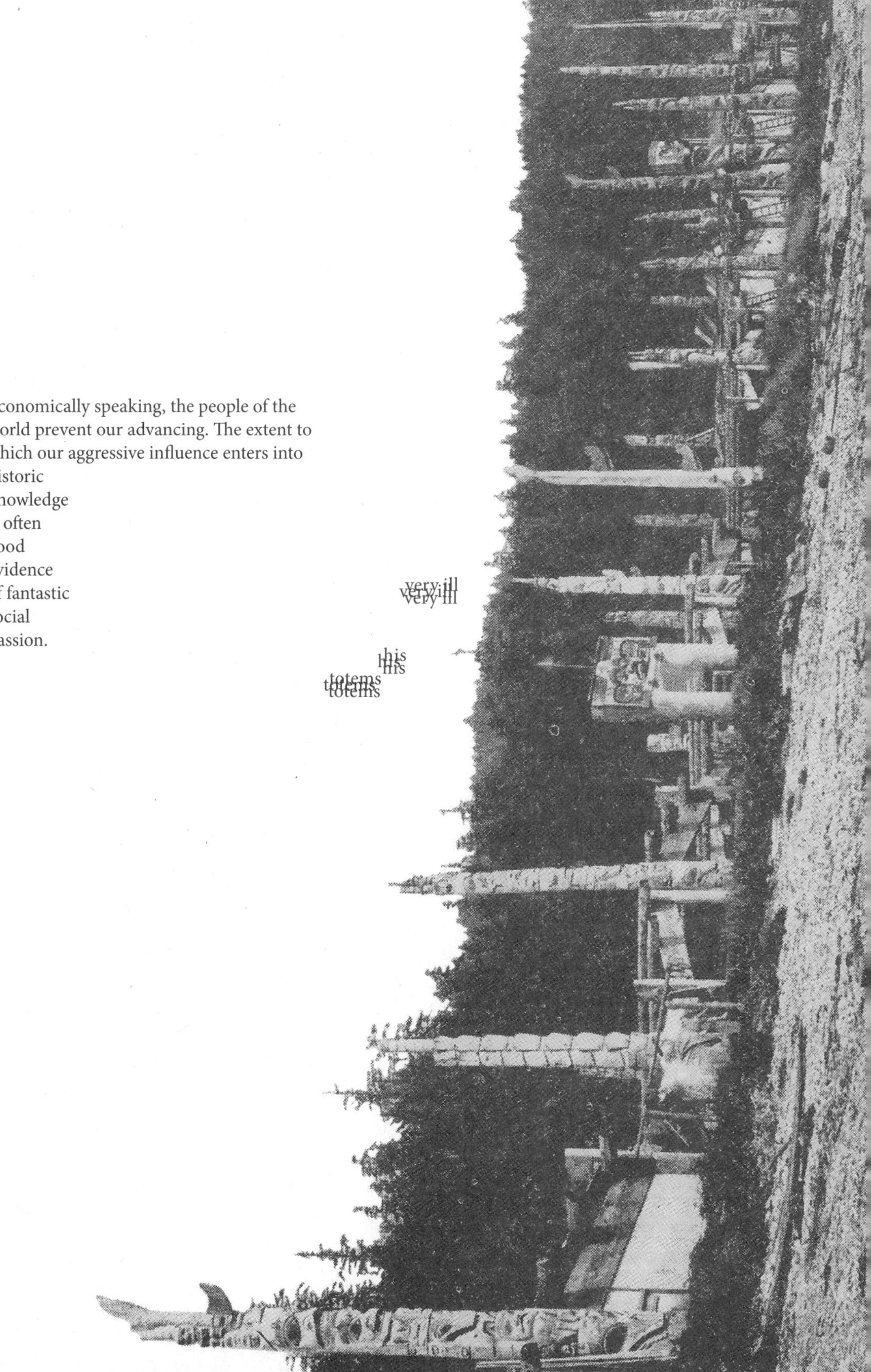

Economically speaking, the people of the world prevent our advancing. The extent to which our aggressive influence enters into
historic
knowledge
is often
good
evidence
of fantastic
social
passion.

very ill

his

totems

The uncertain fractures in the idea of the
soul exist between the body and a new
secondary formation. It is not organized or
independent;
it is stunted,
an accessory.
Yet, it cannot
be exchanged
or observed.

on the
on the

night
night

the
the

ago

In this way,
the to
composite
nature of
culture does
affirm the
purpose of
rudimentary religion. Earlier investigations, however, appear to assume that the mere existence of ritual was nothing of importance.

another
another

in
in

his
his

Many
persons will
deny the
possibility of
the civil
Indian.
Because it is known that the gods of those
limited philosophies are playing rituals into
ritual: the milk of hypothetical histories.

2b

The poet is artificially replaced, amputated by
the instability of simultaneous groupings of
panoptic illusion (compulsory projections of
the human
aesthetic
[impatience
with beauty]).

The cyclicity of these poetics is a negative feature:
massive overemphasis, theory compounded on
theory. Original formations and interjections
are met with
relaxation,
secondary
importance.

Position of
classification
is a struggle.
The whole,
the absurd whole, has itself entered into the
study of poetic tropes—usually directed chiefly
towards metaphor—in all its assuredness.

The subject
then restores
precisely that
opposition
that decodes the necessary political praxis. If and
only if the structure of oppression justifies the
vigilant, universal, socio-synthetic dimension.

There is no duality when constructing a metalanguage. Within the writing, within the represented spatial lines, there is only the act
of interpre-
tation, the
concern for
æsthetic.

One is tempted to struggle with the fixed bond
between the reader and the reading experience,
but any individual, taken almost at random,
would lack the
most basic
competence in
these matters.

A state of
primal unity,
in which we
are bound to
be disappointed, is derived from a
natural analogy—objects cannot be stopped;
meaning conflicts with itself.

The message
was always
the same:
mental
representations of perceived conflict and
consequence, both in terms of politcal reflection,
lack the urgency and performance of culture.

But the divisions of movement (axial visibility,
separated cells) imply formations between
religious, scientific, and ethical systems: those
that are
directed
from body
to body.

Here, science isn't just essential, but the trumpet
of legitimation. All of the effects of truth
converge on the crucial issues of idealism,
meaning, and
interpreation.
All the agents
of knowledge.

As before, the
notes show
us the
evaporation
of cultural equality, the impulse of liberty.
Already the renewed disruption of knowledge
spreads across the globe.

There is no
triumph in
the sunken
view; the
articulation of freedom depends on our engagement
with the fictions of the past. This childhood of
simulation comes equipped with the subjective.

2c

w c n;
p t:
c n
p w t:n; t
c-
c
n c- p t: . t
w n;
c-
n

d h
r t: h
n sd, s p b n t b
d d, dh h c t b
t hr tn r ht: h s gc
n s pms s bp n b n s g
n s d d, h t b
t h n r d, t: h c t b
ss p b n s c g
s g

n d s l g s

s x s l v d

m c t s d t

c t b r l /h t t x s n d d n t w w t s d d

d v n s t s l c

c t m s r c r s /h t b t t d s s, t b t c s h s d d

p t s c r t h /h s t b s g t n t t n t s t w t w

d l s v d t n f r/s t n r n v c s n n d g n t t w s

b r t s s p d w c s r n v t v n c c s

s s p h t f s m x t p s

t c f t s r t l h y s t f c s n g s l g d n t

p d l t h r s n r w d d d d l v

b l l w p d t b x h t f r f l t r w w m d k x c w d h r s g t

w b c k t c t r n; p f v l j n t v n c s h n m w d x d n d d

t c b b x g n r d n t t: n t s w b w d t t s

c n w k w s n b n n g r d c t t y t n w s d p c n

w t: n;twk f t r c- c n s p t t: b l v t t t/h d d

c t r x n d t: p l d

n p n c- w b t l t /h n n n r c w p c t: d t n d t t t n t d

n t d w b t f s n c t s t a r t w r s n v t t

n p t s b t s t t s /h r s c-h s, n c d c d n v c n r p t v

c p b d d, t /h b r r n h p d c w r c w v s g

t n b b d /h t l m h n r w m d

n p s d s t h n n x w r y

c n c s p c d s h c t s f t s c s p h p l c n g

c s d, x v g k s, t m p x t b g

t n b c b d, d s t m h t k s v m x w

b l q c d s n r b c g; h c t p c t p j v c n n t

c m r c t h j g c k c n t d p c b

h l s l d s t l k s s w s d n n g d t k p n b t

g; f p c v n

p l s m d s t v c n t v c n s

n c f l t t n r n c t n g w d

Please
STAY
OUT
of the
Totem Pole
Area
Vancouver Park Board

Sources

Barbeau, Marius. *Totem Poles.* Vol. 1, *Totem Poles According to Crests and Topics.* Ottawa: Department of Resources and Development, National Museum of Canada, 1950.

———. *Totem Poles.* Vol. 2, *Totem Poles According to Location.* Ottawa: Department of Resources and Development, National Museum of Canada, 1950.

Boas, Franz. *A Franz Boas Reader: The Shaping of American Anthropology, 1883–1911.* Edited by George W. Stocking, Jr. Chicago: University of Chicago Press, 1974.

Mauss, Marcel. *A General Theory of Magic.* London: Routledge and Kegan Paul, 1972.

———. *The Gift: The Form and Reason for Exchange in Archaic Societies.* New York: W.W. Norton, 1990.

Mauss, Marcel, and W.S.F. Pickering. *On Prayer.* New York: Durkeim Press/Berghahn Books, 2008.

McQuillan, Martin et al. *Post-Theory: New Directions in Criticism.* Edinburgh: Edinburgh University Press, 1999.

Myres, John Linton. *The Dawn of History.* London: Williams and Norgate, 1927.

Pitt Rivers, Augustus. *The Evolution of Culture, and Other Essays.* Edited by John Linton Myers. London: Clarendon Press, 1906.

Rivkin, Julie, and Michael Ryan, eds. *Literary Theory: An Anthology.* 2nd ed. Malden, MA: Blackwell, 2004.

Sapir, Edward. *Selected Writings of Edward Sapir in Language, Culture, and Personality.* Edited by David Goodman Mandelbaum. Berkley: University of California Press, 1949.

Acknowledgements

My sincerest gratitude goes to the magazines and editors who published earlier versions of these poems: *Canadian Literature,* the *Capilano Review, Contemporary Verse 2, dandelion, filling Station, Geist, OCW Magazine,* and *Poetry Is Dead.*

Thanks to Ray Hsu for his thoughtful questions and generous support throughout the writing of *The Place of Scraps*. Thanks to Daniel Zomparelli for his friendship, encouragement, and belief in my work.

Thanks to Chelsea Novak for letting me destroy the living room in the name of writing poetry – and for everything else.

Thanks to Carolyn Smart, Rita Wong, Wayde Compton, Susan Holbrook, Adam Dickinson, Eric Ostrowidzki, Craig Dworkin, and Christopher Bracken for sharing their thoughts on *The Place of Scraps*. Thanks to Jessica Kluthe for her friendship and for asking great questions.

Thanks to my friends from the University of Alberta for their tireless support, generosity, and encouragement. Thanks to my friends from the University of British Columbia for their keen suggestions and editorial contributions to the first draft of *The Place of Scraps*.

Thanks to Bert Almon for his feedback and guidance. Thanks to Melissa Jacques for her memorable teachings and encouragement. Thanks to Keith Maillard for his insight and enthusiasm. Thanks to Karen Solie for her editorial suggestions and support. Thanks to Elise Partridge for her inspiring correspondence, and thanks to *Arc Poetry Magazine*'s generous poet-in-residence program.

Thanks to UBC's Creative Writing program for giving me the time and space to write. Thanks to the First Nations House of Learning and the Faculty of Graduate Studies for the Aboriginal Graduate Fellowship that provided much-needed financial assistance.

Thanks to Garry Thomas Morse for his unwavering enthusiasm. Thanks to everyone at Talonbooks for believing in my work and for making *The Place of Scraps* a reality.

Thank you for reading this book.

Jordan Abel is a First Nations writer who lives in Vancouver. He holds a BA from the University of Alberta and an MFA from the University of British Columbia. Abel is an editor for *Poetry Is Dead* magazine and the former poetry editor for *PRISM international.* His work has been published in many journals and magazines across Canada, including *Contemporary Verse 2*, the *Capilano Review*, *Prairie Fire*, *dANDelion*, *Geist*, *ARC Poetry Magazine*, *Descant*, *Broken Pencil*, *OCW Magazine*, *filling Station*, *Grain*, and *Canadian Literature*. In early 2013, above/ground Press published his chapbook *Scientia*.